THIS PERISHING WORLD

This Perishing World

New and Selected Poems

David B. Churchill

Pony One Dog Press
Washington, DC

THIS PERISHING WORLD

Cover art: *Leaving Clark's Cove* by Kenneth Layman
Book and cover design: Barbara Shaw

ISBN 978-1-7322882-2-5

First Edition

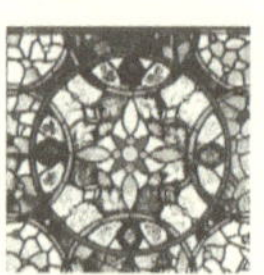

Published by:
Pony One Dog Press
Suite 113
1613 Harvard Street, NW
Washington, DC 20009

Contents

New Poems

Selected Poems

New Poems

Stain Glass

What is this stain
They call "stained" glass,
That anything earthly
Could stain this flower?

Yet how stained *we* were,
us two, father and son—
too long the grape
a stranger to the vine,
too long the bee to the hive,
that no later friendship could revise—

Yet the master loved me,
the least of his apprentices,
and made a window
wherein none look but stainless
should become, and see

cavern lights, one
poet's seated petals,
another's endless bloom—

and a clear rose in every heart …

Neon Christians

Look, see—they come now!
on the beds of trucks
and hoods of cars,
showering beads
and the music of kazoos.

See—throng of tambourines—
they come like crickets,
chirupping at the garden gate,
outlandish in their *lederhosen*,
their bare-chest collar style—

On earth the shadows
of our confident demons;
in heaven, avatars of love . . .
Alas, too soon, too soon,
by ones and twos they filter away,

and I too
wandered alone
down criminal streets,
still afraid of an only smile . . .

Alpaca Circus

They say my poetry's
too difficult to read—
parading images two by two,
but no superior animal
is easier to ride—

for alpacas love bells
and to be loaded with sugar-skulls,
to eat pontifical flowers
and regurgitate the cud,
but try riding them backward
to tame their pride , , ,

So come ye granola bohemians,
Consider the truth:
I have never written an honest word,
but everything stolen,
like one in a deserted arcade,
with a claw-machine
full of scraps of paper—

I took what I could get.

Marijuana Park

There's a park
before our building
and I'm sure it has a name,
but some
who walk through it
call it only Marijuana Park,

and those who avoid it,
a metropolis
of the unhoused;
benches are overgrown
and flagstones crumbling;
the only things
thriving are sparrows.

Too soon the leaves descend;
the architecture
of the sky appears,
lets the wind
through every crack.
Crumbs grow scarce.
Some will not be here
come spring.

On the Dedication of the Emancipation and Freedom Monument

Richmond, Virginia 9/22/21

I went down lately
to Richmond,
a city in Virginia,
with Barbara,
daughter of Peg,

to see a new statue
they had,
and where they had placed it,
it being now
the first time
they unveiled it,

and found it
in a nondescript place,
the anticlimactic
of a thin crowd,
a loose drumbeat
of rain,
speeches nobody listens to,
and a woman

holding the meaning of a constitution
aloft,
written down
in plain words

what the soul
of a people should be,
for those who
forgot,

and I thought,
this woman,
should stand
on the dome of the capitol,
repetition of liberty.

Fountains of the Kennedy Center

Washington, D.C.

I have always admired
the fountains
of this alabaster ark,
loaded with two
of every cello
and ready for space,

that had always seemed
watery conifers,
but are suddenly different
today, and that
has changed something.

Already when it opened
I was thralled
by the fountains
of this improbable monument,
detached from the city
on every side,
that doesn't care
if you can't reach it,
or if tourists don't come,

because I saw things
in the water:
as the waves went up,
frolics of the mind

appeared,
like translucent
frills on a holiday tree,

scenes of domestic
improvements
at first—
relaxing in a tie,
serving dinner with pearls on,

then things
that troubled me,
as if at the bottom
an indistinct refuse,
break-out
lunch counters,
bath of fire-hose
and guardsmen
removing their gloves,

then certain youthful men,
and women
with strange arch faces
as if in brash disguise,
that the water
bore up and dignified,

and I wondered
at the things that collect

when a fountain's
turned off,

and the water broke
and fell back
and new images appeared,
new and again new,
up and always up,

borne up into pure sun . . .
And I with them,
and you would be too,
had you a mind
to see them—

People coming up
can know,
and people who just watch
can know,
and now I know,
for the first time saw
the weight
of that dreadful
downward rush,
that people
always know
what they don't want to know.

End-of-Days

Already we know
the sky of Hiroshima
rolled up,

meanwhile in Deutschland
four horses
appeared
in the smoke of a chimney,

so what has come now
in this burning
of trees,
this raging of sky,

those marionettes
of hate
on the capitol steps,
this anger of humans and nature?

Behold, one people
neatly divided,
some on one side,
the rest on another,

justice manifest
in the way they divided,
led by a man
with admirable horns,

and on their foreheads
"God is Truth"
as they lock-step by
down a darkening slope,
the end-time
returned for its children.

O People of Wisdom

People have asked me
O man of words,
why when you love
swimming so much,
do you hate getting wet?

And others have asked me
O man of words,
when you decry
life everlasting
without the people you love,
why, with respect
to yourself,
so chary of company?

Still others have asked me
O man of words,
when existence itself is
rendered unreal,
closed in like a wall,
why not worth describing,
this custodial scenery?

My answer is this,
O people of wisdom,
why am I silent
about our present situation,
so many trusting

in snake-oil and horse-piss,
railing against
science . . . ?

Buddhism in a Strand of Hair

I don't know much
about Buddhism
but I do know
I shouldn't have had hair
if it's passed
matrilineally,
whose father was bald,

who let me swing on his leg,
and when I asked
where his hair was,
looked me in the eye
and said the wind blew it off,

and I inherited his wit,
but grew up to be
a man of hair,
yet never liked it much,
thick and straight,
like living under a hay-stack,

and now the same wind
is blowing on me,
just when I finally
got it under control—
and I'm surprised to discover
what a part of me
it's become,
like my fingers and toes

or my name . . .
Perhaps I'll take
my grandfather's name,
a bald Chester Goss,

or any name at all,
for names are like air,
you don't know
it's there
until you don't have any,

so if Buddhists
have a god,
say to him for me,
please Lord,
don't let him be nameless,
don't let him be air.

Summer, 2021

The heat
is a blister on the earth.
Athletes fall
dead and their coaches
are blamed.

Children playing
in fountains
are scalded
and shade,
emptied of substance,
now only a notion
of itself,
no longer able
to even cool eyes.

I am not a
summer-loving man
but I miss
the summers of old,
those long-lasting
days, diving
for coins at the pool,
evenings
at Jimmy Cone's . . .

Sunday Morning

August 1st 2021 10 am

It must have rained
during the night,
protected patches
still wet,
but something dried up
all the gasoline
because no cars were about,
the streets at peace;

only walkers were out
with family
members Zelda and Sean
on their leashes,
no more dog
names of Lady and Duke,

and people walking themselves,
like me,
reveling in the summerly
coolness,
though the humidity
was up,
tricked out
in their walking togs,
too humid for jogging,

more people walking
than were ever in churches . . .
But exercise
is a better than prayer,
and walking
a form of meditation,
for fitness is a friendly god,
though one illness
he still gives to the fit.
Then his face
is as empty as empty pews.

Now I am old.
I only walk
to stay in practice,
though my legs
still carry me
faster than my body
wants to go.
Looking back,
I can say
I've come a long way . . .
I can't say I've gotten far.

But I remember being young,
when walking
was a holy act,
always going somewhere,
conscious

of the rushing wind,
unaware
of any ground
beneath my feet,

with just a downy
touch of sorrow
to conclude,
as only the young conclude:
walking the streets,
something
you can only do alone.

The Carpenter

He could read, but
didn't need to:
he knew the Servant Songs
by heart.
People said he had a faraway
look in his eyes
as though you
were a new verse to learn.

Long have I sought but
never found
the written moment:
whether a voice spoke
or a wind blew
a little whirligig of dust
across his path,
when he decided
to lay down his tools
and seek harder wood—

Sought—and found these,
a few things that need to be found:
that men have traded half-truths
for the certainty of science,
and where science is silent,
no truth at all—
and all we have are pieces,

boarded-up streets
and crumbling store-fronts,
and a piece of carpentry

I wish we still knew,
one doesn't tear down a house
to replace the porch—

So when the Carpenter comes
and reads the verse in *my* face,
let Him see
that though I'm still working
on the porch,
my house is still standing . . .

Eden

He spoke to animals but
animals couldn't answer,
he spoke to men but
men ignored him,
he spoke to the children but
the children ran away:
his daughter was lost.

See, there—at the foot of the tree—
a circle of stones she placed
to calm the dark
like a circle of friends, and
there—three sticks on the ground,
an imaginary family
that would soon come to find her—
and there—a small shoe,
and there, a sock . . .

But this ocean of green, this
new world forest too vast,
Only the Indians
who track the wild things
know the ways of the things
that hide in its boughs.
Maybe the Indians
had found her already,
were raising her as their own . . .

Perhaps she would learn
where the best clovers were found,
the coldest streams, the
most sheltering ground,
and through their murmuring unities
she would at least find herself,
and maybe
a little about him . . .

But his patience is like the forest,
an ocean of green
where nothing dies but soon regrows,
and soon . . . now soon
the covering leaves will give a shake
and she will run to his arms . . .

Words for Brandy

5/2/1944 – 7/10/2021

It wasn't the drugs.
The drugs were like
candy on frosting.
To be alive was to be high.

We were like trees
that blossomed first,
then bore fruit,
and watched it drop
misshaped by drought,
not fit to eat.

We hear now
how Jesus promised,
that not all sleep
but shall be awakened,
and be sensible
with donations,
but not much
in the way of flowers.

But I say to you
as I touch your urn,
Brandy, remember me.
I will remember you.

The Muse

Come sweet muse,
let me see your face—
whether body-rub girl or beautiful boy,
old man or crone—
while I yet have a living's
power to see,
like a scimitar on a sultan's belt,
who rests his eyes
in the shade of an oasis . . .

I wanted to serve
the hand of all gifts,
but what can a hand
that only writes out orders and receipts do?
I wanted to hang by one hand,
save a falling child with the other.

In astonishment I watch
my hand write these words:
"Living is free."
Deeds come due but pen and paper are free.
And again in astonishment
new words appear:
"Gifts are love's grace.
Grace has no cost."

Still like that Arab's blade
gratitude is a torment—

Yet now the same hand holds a cup
and a gentle voice says come,
drink, rest your eyes
in the shade as I do,
think not of that blade for a while . . .

slip into your true shape
as I slip into mine—
You too are a muse
and need to say good bye . . .

A Farewell to Poetry

O how beautiful were your tents,
your campsites, O mysterious friend!
You did not leave me—
You left the world.

Not like a blind man
stumbling down a mountain,
heart full of burning letters,
the whole silent desert like a listening ear—

It is a young man's nature
to think his gifts unique,
an old man's nature
to see the wholes of things—

And step out on a winter's night,
and find a new worship,
every man a prophet,
talking to himself.

As I Lay Dying (1)

Nothing happens for the dead,
but everything stops—
no, not anything,
but only by the living
can anything be done.

Even the deaths of desperate men
affect nothing in the world
except by living—
New civilations
do not arise overnight,
nor are wars started
except by living men.

But now how cheerful are they
who come to visit
this dying man,
like the Romans
bringing feasts
to the houses of the already gone,
smashing their toasts
in the still-wet walls
of walled-up doors—

How I wish *this* throng departed
that keeps me here,
for I am tired and have
lived enough.
Tell them I love them but must sleep—

And let come the winter wind
to touch me with its gentle frost,
though a thousand summers
scorch me . . .

As I Lay Dying (2)

Come, bring the mask.
The air grows short.
Try to breathe less.
Leave a little extra for a dying man.

Come, bring the pills.
The bedsheets gnaw at me.
Finish the pleasure—use it all.
I ask only the blessings of oblivion.

What's it like to die?
how would I know?
Like a nurse
who brooks no resistance
giving a sponge-bath,
life strips every comfort,
reveals its hard truth.

This is the hardest part,
the long waiting.
That heart of yours
you took such good care of—
I count its beats now,
the hard center of everything . . .

The Last Cicada

Brood X

I believe I saw the last cicada,
come weaving
out of a grove of trees,
careening over my car
under a sky
that late drilled with its song,
but now is silent.

Cicadas aren't blind
but they fly as if they were;
this one seemed
disoriented by something,
the way he veered—
They fly to their soul-mates
guided by sound,
and now it's gone.

What to make of this sad
new world, so still
you can hear your own blood
ringing in your ears?
My last day of life
will be like a cicada.

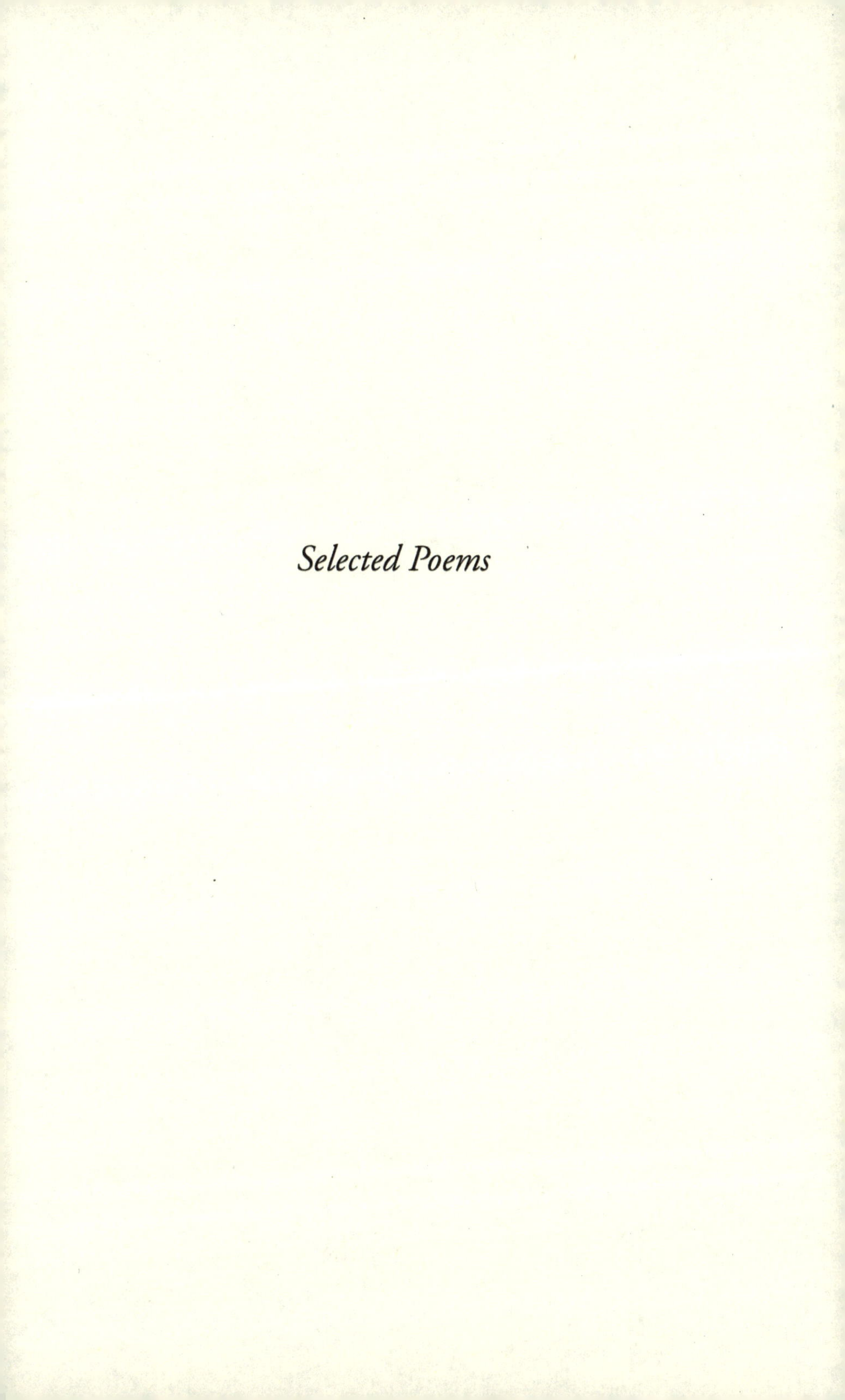

Selected Poems

Kite Sky

6th Street & Boardwalk,
Ocean City, Maryland, 2015

The sky was crowded—
it looked like a Times Square
of kites in the air . . .
But you couldn't look up;
you'd be knocked down

by the crowd on the shore,
shuffling along,
sunburned and bored,
wondering how joy
had eluded them again . . .

Still I saw what the wind
that blows here
from Florida conceals,
when its soul slips clear
and reveals itself . . .

Would that I could be here
a morning in May,
when the wind is still
cold, and no summer sounds
tamp down the surf,

to watch how like sailors
they get those things up—

Perhaps then I would think
differently
of the winds in *our* lives,

if we could see the colorful
parasails they hide—
or get a desire
like one of these seamen,
to unfurl a spinner
on a blustery day,
and celebrate the sky . . .

Bluebottle

The wind blew him in,
a scarab of the air,
all hand polished gold
and metallic green—

Till he fetched up
at a drift-net
in an opposite window,
and there came to grief;

yet I could still praise
the sufficiency of things,
how to find all the
dung-heaps and stables
of the world

with only two navigational
rules:
go where the wind goes
and steer for the sun.

End-of-Summer

We dress in the dark now,
moving around each other
on familiar pinions,
the train sound closer
from the distant cut,

through clairvoyant air.
I count shirts, wondering
if I have enough: we're
in an appraising mood,
seeing what needs mending,

what can be made do with.
The breathing of the children
seems more fragile now,
before we wake them;
in the street

cars start and blow away,
mechanical fluff.
The first touches
of rust are on the trees.

Wherein I Address the Problem of Suffering

I did not know, then,
how blessed I would be,
many years later,
but I should have known better—

There is no comfort
the living can offer
the dying.

So perhaps it was
more for myself
that I watched him pace
the impersonal room
in his golden slippers,
fretting like the child
he still seemed,

as though he already felt
the nurses tightening
their knots
on the trash bag
that would hold his remains
in a week,

and told him
suffering was energy
for change—

And for myself too
that in my mind
I stood at some nameless
siding and saw boxcars
covered in frost,
as if abandoned—
except for the padlocks,

and felt the weight
of a multitude
confined within,

and told them
it is through suffering
God draws us
to Him—

No—I comfort no one
with words.
I have no aide to give.
I come empty-handed
to suffering,

nor do I believe
those who suffer
should also find meaning
in their suffering,
as if it weren't enough
that they suffer,

but must make it
make sense as well.

I take note only of this,
the price we pay
for the gift of love,
our love
for one another,
is the costliest gift of all.

But I will not despair.
I will summon
the guard
to unlock the door of this car—

I will only despair
if there is no room
for one more.

www.ingramcontent.com/pod-product-compliance
Lightning Source LLC
LaVergne TN
LVHW050947080826
845145LV00004B/1439
* 9 7 8 1 7 3 2 2 8 8 2 2 5 *